junkstyle

junkstyle

Melanie Molesworth

photography by
Tom Leighton

RYLAND
PETERS
& SMALL

LONDON NEW YORK

Designer **Luana Gobbo**
Senior editor **Henrietta Heald**
Production **Patricia Harrington**
Editorial director **Julia Charles**

Text by **Melanie Molesworth** and
Alice Westgate

First published in the USA in 1998
This compact edition published in 2006 by
Ryland Peters & Small, Inc.
519 Broadway
5th Floor
New York, NY 10012
www.rylandpeters.com

ISBN-10: 1-84597-095-0
ISBN-13: 978-1-84597-095-6

A CIP record for this book is available
from the Library of Congress.

Printed in China.

contents

introduction

TREASURE HUNTING
this page
Great sources of junk style include secondhand stores, such as the brocantes found in France, and country antiques fairs.

A CLASSIC FIND
left
A Lloyd Loom-style sofa fits in anywhere. A fresh coat of white paint and a simple milk-colored canvas slipcover give an instant update.

Demonstrating beyond doubt that one person's junk is someone else's treasure, this book all about doing new, unexpected, stylish things with objects that might otherwise be forgotten or thrown away. It values possessions that have been loved in an earlier life above those that are pristine and soulless, and it shows that cracks, chips, and blemishes can be part of an item's attraction and proof of its uniqueness.

Although the word "junk" may describe anything that has been discarded, some so-called trash is too good to be consigned to dumpsters. Many pieces cry out to be recycled and reintegrated into our homes. Discerning devotees of junk style pick these pieces from among the clutter, upgrade them, and incorporate their timeless qualities into their lives.

The photographs in this book depict real homes filled with many examples of recycled pieces that are unfailingly chic and elegant. Their owners have embraced the idea of junk collecting so wholeheartedly that they spend a large part of their weekends searching for other objects distinguished by an irresistible faded beauty. For these adherents of junk style, devising new uses in their own homes for items discarded by others has become a way of life. Indeed, much of the appeal of this look is that you cannot simply go and buy it off the shelf. The hunt itself usually constitutes half the fun.

Flea markets, antiques fairs, yard sales, office clearance sales, auctions, thrift shops, secondhand stores, and architectural salvage yards all reveal finds from the exceptional to the ordinary. Each source of junk style is

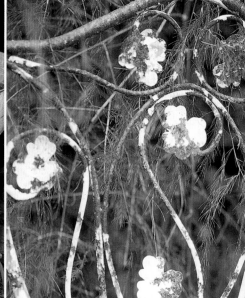

1500 M² de brocante

GOLD AND DROSS
this page
Never forget that there is a fine balance to be struck between being the first to pick a bargain and being the idiot who goes home with a dud.

SPOTTING POTENTIAL
opposite
Before buying any piece for your home, imagine where you might put it. Think beyond traditional uses—a metal bucket could hold firewood, for example.

unpredictable and offers its own secrets: what you end up with depends on where you choose to look, the time when you arrive at your hunting ground, and what your tastes are.

You don't need the skills of a knowledgeable antiques dealer to pick up bargains. The secret is to look for features that particularly appeal to you—a texture, a subtly aged color, skillful craftsmanship, a decorative flourish, or an object's practicality—and to make a purchase based on esthetic considerations, not on price or provenance. Salvaged items sourced with care, restored with love, and introduced to your home with flair will always be its most interesting and expressive pieces.

Don't be afraid to put a contemporary spin on whatever you find, combining old with new in ways that reflect your own personal style. Happy hunting!

inspirational
FINDS

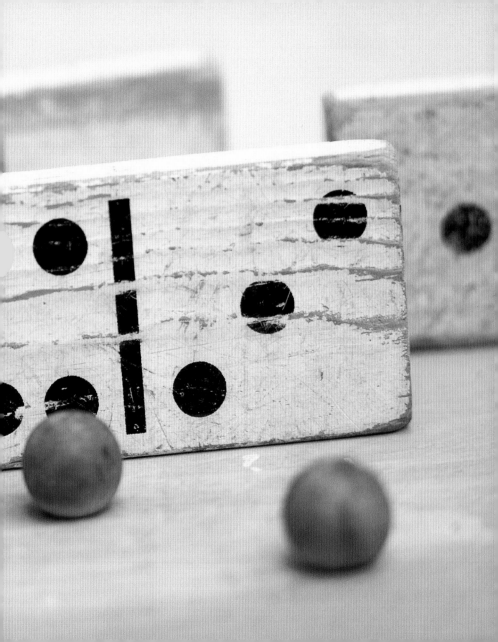

color

The most successful foil for junk style is undoubtedly white or cream. The sheer simplicity of white and its clean, timeless look provide the perfect contemporary background for any type of junk furniture, from polished dark wood tables to classic 1950s couches in jazzily colored slipcovers.

A judicious injection of strong color as an accent on paintwork can add vibrancy to an otherwise cool scheme. But choosing the right shade is vital. Harsh tones can overpower the

WARM EFFECT right
Yellow and cream walls provide a sympathetic backdrop to distinctively shaped furniture finds.

HIGHLIGHTS far right
A single strong color on the ceiling and the window frame gives this bathroom an edge.

subtlety of natural materials and dominate organic pigments that have been gradually dulled by the bleaching effect of the sun and a lifetime of wear and tear. Muted shades that mimic the natural effects of aging, such as pale pastels or earthy terracotta tones, can offer the best complement.

MUTED SHADES right

A color scheme can dictate the mood of a room. The calm, restful atmosphere of this old Long Island barn is enhanced by the subtle shades chosen for the paint on the walls and the simple furniture.

METALLICS left

A Paris apartment has been brought up-to-date with a coat of white paint and an eclectic mixture of metal furniture. The pickled finish on the old beams and floorboards echoes the chalky patina of weathered metal.

HOT HUES right

Bright jazzy colors were the epitome of 1950s style. Here, classic Robin Day chairs in burnt orange sit alongside other 1950s furniture.

SNAZZY STORAGE left and below

Imaginative use of paint turns simple cupboard doors into distinctive decorative features.

surfaces

Surfaces touched by the gentle process of aging are something special that you inherit rather than buy—which is why the flaws characteristic of junk furniture and other salvaged items are so precious.

Peeling wallpaper, roughly plastered walls, exposed bricks, flaking paint on a door, a rusty headboard, some worn-out rugs, a bare wood tabletop, and flagstones polished by centuries of footsteps—all these elements should be cherished because many years of use have made them that way.

In recognition of the value inherent in age, crumbling walls can be left undecorated, the cracked or dusty bare plaster setting the tone for the surroundings in which you can display your junk-shop finds. When it comes to flooring, simplicity is the best approach. Bare boards, sanded down and then either polished with beeswax or pickled for a paler, more contemporary look, are an economical and practical option for virtually every room.

PEELING PAPER above
A hallway with remnants of 1950s wallpaper frames a casual still life of garden paraphernalia.

THE ROUGH WITH THE SMOOTH opposite
Cracked tiles make a practical floor; a rough wall with a road sign brings the outside in; old floorboards are updated; years of peeled paint give an inimitable effect.

Explore architectural salvage yards for discarded flagstones and tiles—and reclaim them. Ceramic tiles bought in small batches might not be enough to cover a whole floor, but they can be incorporated into larger-scale designs, or used to create a fire-surround or make a border around a sink. Cracked or incomplete tiles are useful, too; they can be broken up and laid down to tessellate an area of floor for the ultimate in waste not, want not.

On walls, layers of old wallpaper and paint can be partially scraped back to reveal the decors chosen by generations of previous occupants. Alternatively, you might chance upon some unopened rolls of old wallpaper—in an estate sale, for example—and decide to use them to conjure up the style of another era.

TEXTURAL MÉLANGE
right
This bedroom wall has been left unrenovated, so the overall look is a collage of textures.

PATTERN ON PATTERN
far right
Flaking 19th-century wallpaper clings to the walls alongside layers of old paint and plaster.

furniture

Whether you are looking for things that are handsome or quirky, decorative or functional, antique or contemporary, industrial or domestic—or a mixture of many styles—the joy of junk furniture is that there is something somewhere to appeal to everyone. And a house full of junk furniture has a timeless feel, so scour sales, antique shops and flea markets for pieces that fit in with your home's unique character.

As you become accustomed to shopping in this sort of environment—where a beautiful cabinet might be found hiding beneath a pile of old tea chests—you will grow increasingly adept at distinguishing the interesting and special from the dull and mundane.

SIXTIES STYLE
opposite, left

This swivel chair was bought inexpensively from an office-furnitre warehouse.

GEOMETRIC LINES
opposite, right

The distinctively angular lines of a classic Robin Day armchair create a sharp, boxy shape.

OUTSIDE IN
this page

A weathered garden bench was chosen for its simple curved lines and crusted-paint surface.

PLEASE BE SEATED
left and below
*Raffia chairs are placed
to take advantage of the
sea view; a folding chair
serves as a garden table.*

ALL TYPES opposite,
clockwise from top left
*An old rocker sits on
a beachhouse deck; a
slatted French folding
chair makes a spare seat
for an impromptu guest;
a well-worn chair waits
outside a thrift store
for a loving buyer;
fancy metal seats are
displayed for sale in a
junk lovers' paradise.*

chairs

Junk shops and flea markets are usually filled with chairs that have stood the test of time. Whether your heart's desire is an assortment of seating for a dining room, a dressing-table stool, some metal garden furniture, or a cozy armchair, you are almost certain to strike it lucky. Try each piece for size before you buy, and look for indications that the chair has been comfortable enough to have been well used in the past—the sagging seat of an armchair or a wooden armrest that shines from years of use are both good signs.

If the basic character of the piece is right, quick and easy alterations such as adding a new cover, a simple fabric throw, or some plump pillows will hide any major faults.

SLATTED STYLE
this page
A casual arrangement of furniture borrowed from the garden looks surprisingly elegant in an Amsterdam loft.

PARK CHAIRS
opposite, left and right
Metal-framed wooden chairs such as these, on show at an antiques fair, can make a stylish set of dining chairs.

It is rare to come across a complete set of matching dining chairs or kitchen chairs in a thrift store, so rather than search in vain, consider buying an assortment of single chairs individually, as and when you see them, and gradually build up an idiosyncratic selection of your own.

Look for examples that have arms and gently sloping high backs for ultimate comfort as you dine, and make tie-on seat cushions from scraps of fabric from the flea market to soften their look as well as their feel. You will probably find that your guests are so comfortable that they will want to linger around the table long after the meal is over.

Wicker tub chairs and metal garden chairs—especially folding slatted ones that can be stored flat and then pressed into service if you have unexpected guests—are all worth considering, along with more conventional ladderbacks. Old wooden chairs taken from old meeting halls and schoolrooms often crop up in thrift stores alongside tall

SOLIDITY left

Some chairs, such as this chunky, box-seated example, are so sturdily constructed that they clearly have years of useful life left in them.

VERSATILITY
below left

Placed at convenient points, chairs can make useful extra surfaces.

ELEGANCE right

This pale wooden chair is placed in the best light to show off its glowing color and fine curves.

laboratory stools and rush-seated café chairs. All are perfect for kitchen seating since they are particularly sturdily made and often stackable—an asset if you are short of space.

Elegant one-of-a-kind items such as rockers and woven Lloyd Loom chairs will be perfectly at home in a bedroom or bathroom, creating a quiet corner in which to relax.

For workrooms and studies, office-furniture clearance sales are a good source of seating—adjustable architects' chairs and leather swivel chairs are practical as well as being better-looking than modern options. Make sure you buy one that is the correct height for use with your desk so you will be able to work in comfort as well as style.

CHARACTER inset

You may fall in love with some chairs on account of a detail such as a studded leather seat.

KITSCH main picture

An 1950s chair is the focal point in a corner of this otherwise minimally decorated apartment.

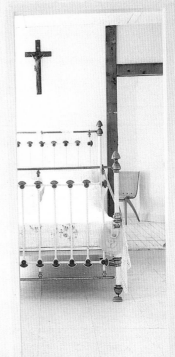

benches
and sofas

A new sofa is expensive, so a junk-store alternative, even if it needs a few repairs, can be an exceptional bargain. Metal-framed daybeds, benches and chaises longues are also much sought because they are sociable pieces of furniture that give a room a relaxed and casual air, especially when piled high with an inviting assortment of pillows or strewn with an old rug or kilim.

A generous seating arrangement is a must in the living room—but is also wonderful in the sort of kitchen that is the hub of family life, a quiet bedroom where you might retreat with a book, a corner of a roomy bathroom, or as a much-needed place of rest in a study.

Whichever part of the house the sofa is destined for, comfort should be your priority when you are on the lookout for the best buys. Sprawl on a sofa before

SACKCLOTH left
Old French flour sacks have been used to make cushion covers for a pretty bench. The covers are designed in such a way as to set off the stitched strip and logo.

REINVENTING THE WHEEL above
An old cartwheel, which was rescued at a sale of redundant farming implements, becomes a work of art when placed in an interior setting.

you buy to check it is as comfortable as it is good-looking. To make sure that wooden, wicker, and metal-framed benches meet the same criteria, buy and attach some feather-filled squab cushions. The bench can then be used as overflow seating in the sitting room or as space-saving seating alongside a rectangular dining table—perfect for children to use at family meals.

Leather-covered couches age well and are lucky flea-market finds that may need only the odd patch here and there to make them serviceable. Along with classic Knoles and Chesterfields, they are the ultimate in shabby chic.

To hide leaking stuffing or a cover that is too worn to leave on show, make some slipcovers from a fabric that will complement the couch's faded look or shroud the whole thing in a large swathe of cloth; ignore the folds and creases and simply tuck in the edges. Look for faded curtains, sacking cloth, and bedspreads with a lived-in look, and your "new" upholstery will not detract from the couch's dated charm.

COVER STORY left

*Sturdy cream linen
sheets help protect a
generous sofa from the
rigors of family life in
this Dutch living room.*

CREASED UP above

*As long as the
framework is sound, any
old couch can be given
a new lease on life with
a simple cream cover.*

tables

Forget convention and use flea-market finds ranging from old cable reels to large trunks as tables. Add a scrubbed plank bench, a simple trestle, or a delicate wirework console— and you'll realize that junk stores can provide every surface you will ever need, from dining tables and bedside cabinets to makeshift desks.

For kitchens, it's hard to beat old pine refectory tables, which are easy to find in all shapes and sizes. They are

very practical, and with a thick coat of tough varnish, can withstand the effect of hot pans as well as the children's crayons. Choose the biggest refectory table your kitchen can take, since it will probably be used for paperwork, hobbies, and reading the newspaper as well as for dining and food preparation.

A better solution than a refectory table in a limited space is a drop-leaf table, which can accommodate larger gatherings of people when necessary, while tables with drawers are useful for additional storage. Small steel-topped tables and butchers blocks can provide extra work surfaces when space is at a premium.

Even if your kitchen is small, keep an eye out for an elegant marble-topped café table with cast-iron legs or a wicker side table that will fit snugly into a corner and be big enough for two people to eat there comfortably.

A small table in the hallway is useful as a surface for keys and mail or as a place to put a lamp or display a vase of fresh flowers for an instant welcome.

BRIGHT WHITE
opposite
White unifies an eclectic mix of junk furniture for a 1990s look. The fluted table legs contrast with the cool swivel chairs.

SWEET DREAMS
above
An old garden table with twisted metal legs works just as well beside a bed as it did surrounded by chairs on the porch.

Look for an unusual piece of furniture to make a striking first impression: for example, a sewing-machine bench, an ornate metal-framed table with a glass top, or a decorative wooden console will establish the junk-style look as soon as you step inside the front door.

Occasional tables are indispensable in living rooms as surfaces for books, magazines, or trays, for example, so search secondhand stores and scour garage sales for anything from small wooden stools and folding butler's tray tables to wooden tea trolleys and stacking coffee tables.

Many of these options can also be useful in bedrooms in preference to conventional matching cabinets, or in the bathroom piled with fresh linens or baskets of soaps.

If you find a table at a flea market that really is past its best for interior use but still has some quality about it that appeals to you, there is a good chance that it will come in handy in the yard or potting shed as a plant stand or workbench.

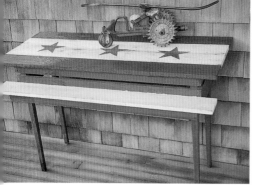

RECYCLING
this page
*A huge cable wheel
becomes a fashion
designer's work table
in a Paris apartment.*

PEDAL POWER
opposite, above
*A sewing-machine stand
complete with foot pedal
makes an unusual side
table in a rustic space.*

STARS AND STRIPES
opposite, below
*National pride obviously
dictated the decoration
for this brightly painted,
two-tier table.*

fabrics

Many junk stores are full of old textiles such as curtains, bed linens, blankets, quilts, lace, mattress tickings, and fabric remnants of all sizes in innumerable colors, weights, textures, and patterns. The inimitable look and feel of faded chintz, old velvet, time-softened linens, and kitsch prints will make an interior feel snug and lived in, so include a variety of these fabrics in your junk-style room designs, combining them with contemporary pieces if you like.

Use more precious pieces sparingly in a position where they can take pride of place, and allow less expensive ones to hang in generous folds. Vintage fabrics can be patched or left threadbare and unironed to imbue your surroundings with an air of relaxed living.

TICKING OVER left
There is a huge choice of traditional mattress tickings; a variety of stripes and colors often work well together.

PIANO COVER right
A pretty striped cotton in French blue contrasts with blue checks on the chair and disguises a piano in this small room.

LADDER OF SUCCESS above
An old ladder simply propped up against a wall makes an original towel rod, useful in the bathroom or the kitchen.

A TOUCH OF LACE
below
*Recycled curtains
provide a delicate lacy
undersheet beneath
the top cover.*

RAMBLING ROSES
below right
*Rose-patterned drapes
spread over a dormitory
bed transform the mood
of the room.*

Vintage fabrics have a charm that cannot be replicated by modern materials, however faithful fabric companies may be at reproducing old designs. The fabrics that survive years of good service relatively intact tend to be the durable ones. They are usually made from natural rather than man-made fibers, and they complement the other natural textures, such as wood, that form such an important element of junk style.

The authentic feel of antique linen or lace, or soft woolen blankets that have been washed so many times the nap has worn smooth, more than compensates for a frayed edge or an occasional hole. Paisleys, florals, stripes, and checks are a useful way to bring a splash of pattern to otherwise subtly

VIOLETS above

Subtle florals, such as this 1950s design, can soften an otherwise coolly decorated room.

FLORAL CHARM above left

A country junk store's rummage basket was the source of this pretty bedcover, once a curtain.

decorated rooms. Even the most overblown chintz will look charming rather than overpowering when surrounded by the casual restraint of junk style. So drape dining tables with layers of linen and lace for a touch of faded grandeur, dress beds with antique linens, soft quilts, and feather-filled pillows, cover couches and chairs with fabrics such as

PURE WHITE
left and below

All-white bed linen lends a monastic feel to a room. For extra warmth, follow the example of the owner of this 19th-century wrought-iron traveling bed and add woolen blankets.

PICNIC CHECKS
right

Faded blankets in contrasting pastels were used to reupholster this pair of classic armchairs with rounded arms; they are soft, comfortable oases in a minimally furnished London loft.

sensual silk, knobbly chenille, starched cotton, and warm wool to enhance their comfortable appeal.

To complement rich vintage textiles, buy new lengths of timeless gingham, striped ticking, muslin, or canvas, and make them up into slipcovers or sew them into borders. These utility fabrics blend well with older, more decorative examples. Try mixing new gingham with a faded floral, pristine ticking with old checks, unbleached cotton with elegant damask, or a length of linen with a panel of antique embroidered lace.

If you are a diehard recycler, you will do what generations have done before you and collect any leftover scraps to make into a patchwork quilt.

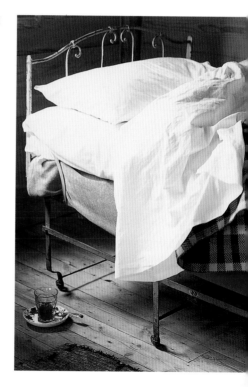

containers
and storage

For innovative storage solutions, junk stores make wonderful hunting grounds. Storage items from boxes and baskets to cabinets and shelving are essential ingredients of any well-organized home, whether you like to keep a minimalist, clean, contemporary look or to fill your home with an array of treasured clutter.

Keep a lookout for both conventional and unusual pieces to house your possessions. Particularly useful finds include wooden crates, enameled tins and bread boxes, medicine chests, baker's racks, butcher's hooks, and an assortment of basketware.

POTS OF STYLE left
Kitchen scales and salt pots sit among storage jars in a monochrome collection from a French country kitchen.

BOXED IN top
A abundance of dents and a rusty, peeling-paint finish simply enhance the charm of these old storage cans.

GREAT CRATES above
These baskets and wine crates, complete with their original lettering, make a relatively cheap but chic storage solution.

small storage

Before the days of mass production and man-made materials, everything from vegetables to soap powder was sold in cans, trays, bags, crates, racks, barrels, boxes, and baskets that were carefully packaged and frequently labeled with beautiful lettering to advertise their contents and the producer's identity. The containers were so durably made that many survive today, often cropping up among the junk at booths and markets after years of being shut away in attics and cellars. All deserve to be given a new lease on life, so buy them to use for storage all around the home. They are far more desirable than the crude replica cans and baskets that are now on the market in response to a revived interest in period pieces.

Wooden grocer's trays and vegetable crates can be used for displaying plants in a conservatory, storing toys in a playroom, growing herbs on a kitchen windowsill, or holding supplies of dried goods in the kitchen. Brightly painted

EGG BOX above
A metal box originally used to store eggs has found a new use as a receptacle for letters and paperwork.

ENAMELWARE right
Popular in the 1930s, enamel kitchenware, including bowls, tureens, and colanders, is still going strong today.

logos, especially ones that reveal an exotic past, are most popular. Old shopping bags, picnic hampers, and fisherman's baskets are covetable for their intricate workmanship as well as their versatility. Fill them with shoes to store under the bed or line them with fabric and use them for laundry.

Enameled cans often appear among kitchen items in junk stores—perhaps labeled "flour" or "sugar," sometimes striped or with colored lids. French versions, for storing *farine* or *sucre*, are especially desired by people wanting to recreate rural Provençal style or faded Parisian chic. A mismatched collection can look wonderful on a kitchen shelf and the cans are as useful today as they were originally.

Metal trunks, old suitcases, and leather collar and hat boxes can be filled with clothes, books, and papers before being piled on top of an armoire or under a dresser to create an attractive display as well as making the most of a limited space and reviving age-old household practice. For bathrooms, search for wooden drying racks, linen chests, and laundry baskets to store towels, and small shelving units, glass bottles, and small baskets for toiletries. Map chests, bookcases of all shapes and sizes, and wooden crates are ideal for books and magazines; they can also be used to hold the accumulations of modern life that add clutter to the clean lines of the junk-style look, while a metal filing cabinet will swallow up household papers, bills, and

WELL DRESSED
above left

A utilitarian metal rod is a perfect makeshift closet, allowing a fine array of secondhand clothes to be placed permanently on show.

INVENTIVE IDEAS
from left to right

A row of wooden birdhouses sits on top of a set of painted drawers; the empty spaces where drawers are missing are used to display favorite objects. Barrels, wicker baskets, and bowls can be recycled to store everything from fresh laundry to fresh garden produce. A collection of books and glassware is displayed enticingly on open shelves.

GARDEN DISPLAY
above

A rickety wooden baker's stand is an attractive addition to a sheltered corner of the yard. It is a convenient place to keep tools and equipment and to display fruit and vegetables freshly picked from the kitchen garden.

documents. Glass-fronted cabinets and open shelves are useful all around the home; look out for old store display furniture, such as large wooden notions display counters with glass-fronted drawers. In the bedroom it's hard to beat freestanding metal clothes rods, blanket chests, and old leather suitcases for original and truly stylish storage.

In awkward spaces such as halls, try pegs, hat stands, drawstring shoe bags and metal shelving. Paneled wooden doors, in plentiful supply at flea markets, can be set over existing alcoves and recesses to make extra cupboards that look as if they have been there for years. Equip them with shelves or rows of hooks and you will have the ideal place to store linen, coats, and household equipment.

KITCHEN CABINET
right
An old-fashioned meat safe is a stylish way to expand kitchen storage.

HERB GARDEN
below
For a handy kitchen garden, drill holes in the base of a wooden crate and plant it with a variety of culinary herbs.

PORTABLE
below left
A shallow-sided crate can be used as an impromptu tray.

cupboards

With a little imagination, the cupboards on sale at flea markets and auctions can provide ingenious storage solutions. For example, a painted metal kitchen cabinet would make a convenient place to store dishes, an armoire could become a pantry, and a small wooden kitchen hutch could find a new role in the bathroom stacked high with towels.

Large cupboards are at a premium in junk shops because they are such practical, handsome additions to the home, especially in the bedroom, where a freestanding, French-

CUPBOARD LOVE
this page
Painted wall cupboards, simple and ornate, can be found in all shapes and sizes at flea markets.

BLENDING IN far left
*Pale, neutral walls make
a perfect background
for this subtly bleached,
metal-trimmed cupboard.*

VERY COOL left
*A classic fridge, stripped
of its enameled surface,
shows off its sleek lines.*

IN THE GARDEN below
*No junk item, not even
an armoire, should be too
precious for outdoor life.*

style armoire or a rough-and-ready pine one can be stylish.
Corner cabinets allow you to make the most of space that
would otherwise be wasted. Details such as carving, ornate
decorative moulding, colored-glass insets, a mirrored front
panel, and attractive hardware make a purchase worthwhile.

Easier to carry back from your junk-store foray are smaller
cupboards, useful for storage throughout the home. Glass-
fronted cabinets are ideal if you are happy to put the contents
on show. Whether you are dealing with cans of baked beans
or your best china pieces, arrange them in an appealing way.

Revamping cupboards with new or reclaimed doorknobs,
handles, and decorative and unusual brass or iron hinges,
or even just polishing the existing ones with steel wool, can
work wonders—as can replacing cracked or warped door
panels with etched or clear glass, chicken wire, or a length
of fabric gathered on a wire.

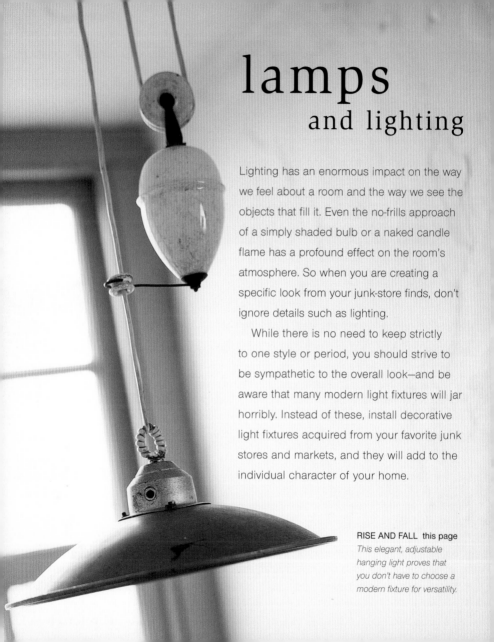

lamps
and lighting

Lighting has an enormous impact on the way we feel about a room and the way we see the objects that fill it. Even the no-frills approach of a simply shaded bulb or a naked candle flame has a profound effect on the room's atmosphere. So when you are creating a specific look from your junk-store finds, don't ignore details such as lighting.

While there is no need to keep strictly to one style or period, you should strive to be sympathetic to the overall look—and be aware that many modern light fixtures will jar horribly. Instead of these, install decorative light fixtures acquired from your favorite junk stores and markets, and they will add to the individual character of your home.

RISE AND FALL this page
This elegant, adjustable hanging light proves that you don't have to choose a modern fixture for versatility.

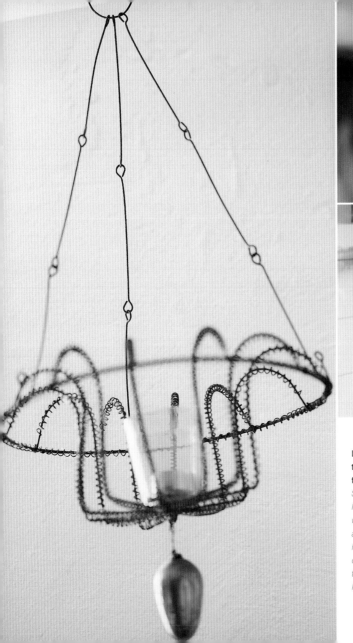

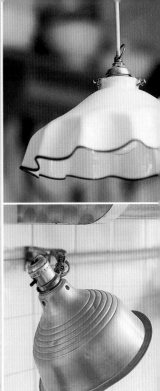

LIGHTS FANTASTIC
this page, clockwise
from left
*Search flea markets for
light fixtures such as
wirework candleholders,
a French glass shade to
hang over a table, or a
clip-on metal spot lamp
that is perfect for task
lighting in the kitchen.*

lamps and lighting **55**

Salvage yards and secondhand outlets are usually well stocked with original light fixtures removed from old houses in the name of modernization. Some of these items are fully functional and can last another lifetime if rescued and reused. Secondhand electric-light fixtures should always be checked and installed by a qualified electrician, so that any worn or damaged wiring or connections can be replaced. Once their safety has been certified, old fixtures can do a more stylish job than their modern equivalents, which are often too high-tech to combine easily with more traditional junk elements.

Candlelight creates a warmth and romance that harmonize well with junk style, so use it as much as possible. Candleholders come in many different forms, from custom-designed containers to old pots and jars adapted for that purpose. For a decorative flourish, old pewter candlesticks, perhaps dented or worn smooth by years of polishing, can be picked up relatively cheaply from among more expensive antiques. Rustic options include storm lanterns, which look great on a mantelpiece or table, but which are also useful outside on summer evenings.

A GOOD SIGN left
As well as buying old lights, you can adapt other junk items to camouflage modern light fittings. French lighting designer Alexis Aufray made this highly original light fitting out of an old rusted-metal road sign. The bulb behind floods the wall with light.

Before you head off on your first foraging expedition, plan the lighting scheme for your entire home, deciding what style of fixtures you want and where they will go. Each room needs something to provide general or ambient lighting—a central hanging light, for example. There should also be individual task lights over desks, beside armchairs, and in kitchens to facilitate studying, reading, or cooking. Finally, you will need

STORM FRONT above
Whether used to light an alfresco meal or simply as outdoor decoration, hurricane lamps are romantic and stylish.

CANDLE LIGHT above
Bulbous storm lanterns are suspended from a beam on wire hangers.

ON THE ROAD right
A roadworker's lamp finds a new use in an Avignon restaurant.

GASLIGHT far right
A mirror reflects the metal wick control of an old gas-light fitting with its original glass lantern.

some sort of accent lighting to draw the eye toward particular items that you wish to highlight, such as a work of art or an attractive collection of objects on display. Lighting to fulfill all these roles —plus any pieces you fall in love with on the spot for their purely decorative qualities and elect to find a place for as soon as you return home—can easily be found by sifting through junk stores.

Finding a colored or plain glass-drop chandelier might well be one of the highlights of your search—with a bit of cleaning and perhaps a replacement

glass drop here and there, it will give off a delicate twinkling light that is grand but never gaudy. Hang it in conventional style over a dining table or somewhere more unusual, such as a bathroom, to give an air of opulence.

Alternatively, you can decide to use a chandelier purely as a beautifully decorative object and not have it wired to the electricity supply for use as a light. If you go for this option, hang the chandelier near a source of natural light such as window so the glass drops catch and reflect the sunlight.

TAKE THE FLOOR
left

An ornate floor lamp set to one side of an open fire makes this an ideal spot to relax with a good book. A model dog offers suitably silent company.

Candelabra make similarly grand statements, but remember that lighted candles should never be left unattended, and that the smoke can stain painted walls and ceilings.

Look out, too, for glass or ceramic uplighters that will wash an entire wall with gentle light, and for elegant standing lamps, with or without their original shades. Pleated shades to fit—silk if you are lucky, paper if you are not—can often be found separately, along with an assortment of other shades in glass, metal, parchment, wicker, or fabric. These can either be paired off with other lamp bases you might find or easily adapted to use with hanging fixtures.

Wall sconces—some incorporating candleholders, others fitted with kitsch, flame-shaped bulbs—are also much sought after, especially wrought-iron models in ornate floral or foliage designs. The best finds are always the classic designs—in this case, adjustable gooseneck desk lamps, tall metal standing lamps with extending arms, and traditional brass picture lights.

A GOOD ANGLE
above
Gooseneck lamps are essential accessories in traditional or modern offices. Their flexible and stylish design has altered little over the years.

CLEAR YOUR DESK
above left
Yard sales are a good source of adjustable desk lamps. Check that the springs are sound before you buy. If they are too tight, the lamp will not budge; if they are too loose, it will flop.

glass, china,
and ceramics

The delicate floral china plates and cut-glass vases that were last cherished by our grandmothers are now fashionable once again and are an integral part of junk style. Think of a cream pitcher filled with flowers, a china bowl planted with hyacinths, a shelf laden with dishes, a table piled with earthenware, or a tea tray set with bone china, and you'll capture the right look. Affordable prices make it easy to build up a collection for daily use or for decoration. Looking through piles of plates, searching for an unusual design, and imagining how a bottle would look when cleaned, adds to the enjoyment.

MIX AND MATCH left
Collect assorted pieces of cheap glassware and flatware for everyday use.

**SOMETHING SPECIAL
above left**
Glass vases, dishes, and cake plates are useful one-of-a-kind purchases.

DECORATION right
Intricately patterned spoons, some tied in a bundle with blue wool, make a still life on a glass dish. Although the flatware is mismatched, the styles are similar enough to result in a harmonious whole.

Gone are the days when we had to have a fully matching dinner service. Now, table settings with character can comprise mismatched plates, odd glasses, and an assortment of flatware. Whether you are hosting a dinner party or just having a few friends for morning coffee, a casual mix of glass and china will make it an easygoing affair.

Tableware makes up only a fraction of the pieces you are likely to come across. If you spot a bowl and pitcher set, a dish, or some hutch china, your junk-shore discoveries could also be used to adorn your bathroom and bedroom. Similarly, bottles and jars that were discarded years ago when the milk, medicine, or ginger ale ran out

SHELF LIFE opposite
Simple wooden shelving is the perfect place to display china plates amassed over 25 years.

FISHY above left
This collection of china is united by a seaside theme, making it witty as well as pretty.

ALL SET above
Among more ordinary china you may be lucky enough to find a complete dinner set.

USER FRIENDLY below
Flea-market finds are not only for show. If you use them for daily meals, you will come to appreciate them to the full.

often find their way back into the home by means of yard sales and estate sales. Use them to display a single flower stem or line them up en masse on a windowsill. Colored glass looks particularly good when it filters shafts of sunlight beside a window, so search for old bottles in vivid shades of cobalt blue, soft aqua, deep green, or glowing amber. Embossed lettering and original labels, plus lids, stoppers, and corks, add to their charm.

IN BLOOM left
Antiques and flowers are combined in Potted Gardens, a New York florist's store.

KEEP IT SIMPLE
opposite, clockwise from top left
Plain glassware often makes a perfect vessel for a floral arrangement; you can display single stems in clear tumblers, for example. An antique cachepot has become home to a simple display of backyard flowers. A row of inexpensive salt shakers has been used to make an eye-catching display on a shelf in a seaside home. Big containers are ideal for large flowers; the narrow neck of this vase easily supports a huge allium.

COCKTAIL KITSCH
top
Plastic glamour-girl swizzle sticks from the 1950s make a perfect match for these modern classic tumblers.

ROSY OUTLOOK
right
For impromptu displays all around the home, fill cut-glass tumblers with seasonal flowers.

collections
and collectibles

Any discovery can provide the starting point for a collection of junk objects—from an array of old tobacco tins to a handful of lead fishing weights. Once you have found something you covet, every subsequent visit to a junk store will have more significance because it might reveal just the thing you have been looking for.

A collection speaks volumes about the person who has amassed it, and quirky and highly idiosyncratic items often become the most obsessively sought. The quest for picture books, pearl buttons, board games, egg whisks, hats, or birdcages can become all-consuming, and when displayed around the home in a decorative and eye-catching way, these objects introduce lovely witty touches.

ARTFUL left and above
*The contents of artist
Yuri Kuper's former barn
in Normandy reveal his
fondness for architectural*

*prints in addition to
quirky objects such as
lock barrels—cherished
for their aesthetic rather
than monetary value.*

BESIDE THE SEA
above right
*This collection of fishing
weights turned up in a
local thrift store.*

TINWARE left
These battered cans are on show in Yuri Kuper's loft home in New York.

HANDIWORK right
Tools become decorative items in their own right when hung on a wall.

GARDEN SHED below
Collector's items may be lying forgotten; search out bell jars, pots, and watering-can sprinklers.

FLAT OUT far right
Choose one type of item—such as an antique flat iron—and look for more wherever you go.

Many other everyday objects are well worth collecting—and can frequently be picked up easily at yard sales. The perennial favorite is old kitchenware, and some covetable equipment and utensils, such as kettles and weighing scales, can earn their keep as well as enlarge your collection if they are still in working order. Garden tools are another popular option, especially old trowels, terracotta pots, and baskets, which can either adorn a sunroom or be pressed back into service. But not everyone who spends hours searching for the perfect piece to augment his or her collection ends up with a house full of clutter. Collecting can be compatible with a desire for a more minimal interior. Whatever look you want to create, be precise: discretion and theming are the keys to making discerning purchases from the myriad junk items available.

A CUT ABOVE left

Show off your cherished treasures behind glass. Dressmakers' tools and a tape measure go on display in two fine jars.

IN STITCHES right

A still life is created from a collection of old sewing paraphernalia— much still in its original delightful packaging.

WELL SPUN left

The natural hues of these old silk threads, some still threaded on factory-sized spools, form another collection based on haberdashery.

decoration
and display

Finding ways to arrange the items you have collected from junk stores and flea markets is enormously enjoyable. The more innovative and creative your displays the better, since they will invite you to look at old objects in a new light and allow you to decorate your home with an interesting and personal touch. For small-scale arrangements, corner cabinets, narrow shelves, small cubbyholes, and old wooden printer's type boxes are tailor-made. Displays of belongings make a room feel lived in, so keep them fresh by changing them whenever the mood takes you—or when a buying trip forces you to move things to make room for another irresistible treasure.

ULTRA MARINE
above left
Flying birds, a wooden sailing boat, and some spades comprise a distinctly nautical display in a seaside home.

HAT STAND left
An old fruit-picking ladder is used to display a collection of hats in artist Charlotte Culot's Provençal home.

STILL LIFE right
Dried seed heads, ceramics, pictures, and shells are the simple ingredients that bring a shelf to life.

HOLY ORDER above

*Religious icons fill a
shrine-like wooden
cupboard in a home
in Amsterdam.*

THREE IN A ROW right

*Simple wooden shovels
are propped up against
the wood-panel wall of
a beach house*

BEACH FINDS far right

*Treasures retrieved from
the seashore have been
used to cover a selection
of small boxes.*

JAGGED above right

*A rusty saw embellished
with wonderful lettering
has been given pride of
place on a white wall.*

Look out for glazed box frames and glass-fronted cabinets to show off tiny trinkets. Especially in the kitchen, larger items can be hung from ceiling racks and wooden clothes dryers. Some successful displays arrange like with like so you can enjoy their similarities. Imagine the effect of seeing a row of identical clear-glass apothecary jars on a bathroom cabinet, or a shelf of spongeware pitchers. Other displays work well because of the juxtaposition of different styles, colors, and textures. You might love the contrast between contemporary ceramics and old porcelain, or between kitsch artificial flowers and brass candlesticks.

GALLERY overleaf

Treasures varying from a life buoy to a battered shoe last can be used for decoration.

found
objects

Junk-style addicts keep their eyes open
for objects of interest wherever they go.
Whether you are spending a lazy day
on a beach, digging in a flowerbed,
or out on a woodland walk, you may
discover a natural wonder or some
man-made object discarded long ago
that can become a treasure in its own
right. Such things are particularly
satisfying to collect since they are close
at hand, easy to find, and—best of all—
absolutely free.

MANTELPIECE
this picture
These skulls were found in the Camargue and in Africa, while the antlers are from Provence.

NATURAL SELECTION
left
A walk in the woods can yield a wealth of natural finds, from feathers to textural stones.

WOOD AND STONE
far left
Interesting pieces of driftwood, wood bowls, and undressed stone surfaces give a natural look in a bathroom.

IN FULL BLOOM
right

An old wooden barrow, complete with its original wheel, has been planted to create an unusual container garden.

IN THE FRAME
this picture

Odd pieces of flatware are mounted on white cardboard and put in secondhand frames.

HIDDEN POTENTIAL
far right

Another wheelbarrow languishes in an outhouse awaiting a similar transformation.

Beachcombing is as much fun for adults recapturing childhood memories as it is for children discovering the joys of the seaside for the first time. Scan the high-water mark and you might find jewellike pieces of sea-smoothed glass washed up alongside delicate feathers, gnarled and twisted lengths of sculptural driftwood, chunks of flint, and maybe a lobster pot or a float.

As they turn over the soil, gardeners are accustomed to unearthing a wealth of interesting objects. Fragments of pottery, perhaps a section of glazed tile, a cup handle, or a section of clay pipe, are all worth keeping. Elsewhere in the yard, old flowerpots and wrought-iron brackets are waiting to be discovered and appreciated. Luckier finds are discarded garden tools, such as rusted rakes and shovels, or even an old wheelbarrow. These can be turned into permanent decorative features in the garden or even brought into the house to be shown off.

flowers

A vase of fresh flowers brings immediate
warmth to an interior space filled with
junk objects. Being relatively short-lived,
floral arrangements provide a graceful
counterpoint to the imperfections and
timelessness of old furniture. Choose
plants in vivid shades to introduce an
intense note that will instantly lift the
spirits. Such an injection of vitality will
probably be particularly welcome in
rooms with neutral schemes.

DELICATE TOUCH
this page
*Plain shapes and clear
glass are the best vehicles
for simple flowers.*

FORMAL OR INFORMAL
left, above and below
*A stemmed bowl makes a
perfect table centerpiece,
while a metal pitcher offers
a more casual display.*

INDOOR GARDEN
far left, small pictures
*Mottle-glazed ceramic pots
are ideal for holding all sorts
of floral specimens, short or
tall; or bring terracotta pots in
from the garden and enjoy
the flowers while they bloom.*

NEW LIFE far left,
above and below
An old metal kettle is
now home to a cluster of
cheerful pansies, while
an enameled jug plays
host to hydrangeas.

WELL CONTAINED
right and below right
Junk discoveries such
as these buckets make
perfect vases—the
more unexpected the
container the better.

SPIKE
left
Plants will be happy in all
manner of containers as
long as they have proper
drainage holes.

PITCHER PERFECT
below
Place a few sprays of the
same flower in different
vases close together for
a charming group.

living with
JUNK

living
and dining

Once you have managed to acquire the best secondhand furniture, fabrics, and accessories you can find, it is time to put all the elements together to create a home that looks good and is easy to live in. There are no rules about making exact matches—or even about using items for the purpose for which they were designed. One pleasure of using junk is that salvaged pieces bring with them some of the character of their former life. But junk style is not an excuse for wallowing in nostalgia, nor does it seek faithfully to recreate replicas of historical interiors. It is a look that is very much of the moment.

Junk-style interiors are fresh and contemporary. The less clutter there

CLASSICS left
Twentieth-century, Le Corbusier-designed chairs mingle happily with more humble flea-market furniture in a Paris apartment.

BASIC NEEDS above
Decoration is minimal in this 17th-century grain store, where no more than an old picnic basket and a couple of casual shirts adorn the walls.

is around, the better able you are to appreciate the clean lines of chairs and tables chosen for their strong shapes.

Often it is a particular texture or color that will have attracted you to a secondhand item in the first place—the glow of aged wood patinated with the scars of previous use, for example, or the jewellike shine of colored glass—so you will want to show off your finds to their best advantage. Spontaneity and a lack of pretension are at the heart of junk style. Whatever pieces you find

KEEPING IT SIMPLE
left and this picture
A rough garden spade
decorates the wall of Yuri
Kuper's New York loft,

while an old pine table
with several mismatched
chairs is well placed to
enjoy the canal view
in Amsterdam.

will speak for themselves, establishing their own unique style and making everyone who enters your living space feel completely and utterly at home.

For a spacious look with restrained adornment, decorate your living and dining areas with white walls and a few selected treasures. For a busier effect, paint them in rich shades and introduce the paintings and quirky *objets d'art* you have picked up over the years.

If there is space for two or even three sofas in your living room, arrange them so that they face one another, perhaps beside a couple of slouchy armchairs, to make a sociable grouping. Despite the variety of shapes and sizes and the different colors and design of the worn upholstery fabrics, the room will feel harmonious since each of the elements in it is laid back and unaffected.

If you are lucky enough to have a fireplace, arrange your sofas and chairs in such a way as to make it the room's focus. Look out for old fireirons, coal scuttles, metal fenders, and screens to set in the hearth to complete the

picture. Other junk purchases such as low footstools and occasional tables, feather-filled scatter cushions, colorful throws, and tartan blankets add comfort and convenience. Search for rag mats and woven hearth rugs to give the room yet another layer of softness.

LONG TABLE above
Charlotte Culot bought her generously sized dining table from a flea market in Ardèche.

EATING OUT above right
Minimal restoration was done when this stylish Avignon restaurant, *called Woolloomooloo, was converted from an old print works.*

RURAL RETREAT right
This reclaimed grain store has been furnished with a charming hotch-potch of finds.

Whether you prefer a separate dining area or tend to eat in the family room or kitchen, every home needs a place set aside for enjoying food. Junk style creates a warm and inviting look that is a far cry from the stuffiness of a formal dining room. No one has to stand on ceremony because the table is rough-and-ready pine rather than polished mahogany, the candlesticks are hand-blown glass rather than solid silver, and the tablecloth is a country-style length of gingham check rather than starched white damask.

Table settings can be as plain or as ornate as you like. At one end of the spectrum is a no-frills approach, with a bare wooden table-top set with plain white china in a mixture of weights and shapes, linen napkins, stainless-steel flatware, chunky glasses, and a pitcher of flowers. For special occasions, old lace can form the backdrop for floral china, assorted bone-handled silver cutlery, elegant cut-glass goblets, and a stemmed crystal dish piled high with fruit as a centerpiece.

ON THE BENCH above
Long benches may have started life as anything from garden furniture to church pews; they are very versatile in dining rooms because they can seat so many people.

WOOD right
The beauty of wooden furniture is that whatever type of wood it is, from pine to oak, and whatever the color, it will always look good with other wooden furniture.

kitchens

People tend to gather in the kitchen because it is a place of warmth, somewhere they can go to enjoy good company as well as nourishment, where conversations, meals, work, food preparation, and leisure activities can all happily take place alongside one another.

TAKE A SEAT
opposite
*Ex-church chairs make
fine kitchen seating.*

KETTLES GALORE
below and left
*Old aluminum items can
be found in abundance.*

Kitchen junk looks at home even in a modern setting. It makes a lovely contrast to stainless-steel stoves and built-in cabinets, and gives authenticity to retro kitchens. If you have a modern streamlined kitchen, you might find yourself choosing fewer junk pieces than you would for a more country-style kitchen, but the junk elements you do include will really stand out against the room's cool, clean lines.

It can be fun to scour markets and salerooms in search of early examples of kitchen equipment. Pieces dating from decades ago, such as meat mincers, coffee grinders, juicers, nutcrackers, and weighing scales with sets of brass or iron weights were often so well designed and sturdily built that they are still going strong today.

Often better looking than many of today's plastic or electronic gadgets, yesterday's household goods are also far more satisfying to use. Old utensils have similar esthetic advantages. Sets of saucepans, tiny metal tea strainers, enameled colanders, ladles, spatulas,

RETRO CHIC left
Designer Roxanne Beis admired the 1940s cupboards she inherited with her Paris flat so much she designed her kitchen around them.

POTS AND PANS above
This matching set of aluminum saucepans with white handles was discovered in a Paris flea market.

rolling pins, and strainers can be suspended from a kitchen shelf, where they are always within easy reach. Keep your eyes open for other hardware that would add character to your kitchen—from thermometers, trays, and canisters to buckets, mops, and brooms.

If you want a traditional country kitchen, enhance the reassuringly familiar look by adding an old refectory table, some unpainted wooden cupboards, a few plain rush-seated chairs or long benches, and the most basic floor covering you can find; bare boards, terracotta tiles, or rush matting would be perfect. Keep the look as uncomplicated and utilitarian as possible. Copper pans can be hung up for decoration

BACK TO BASICS
left
This simply furnished barn deep in the Dutch countryside takes guests back to simpler times.

HEART OF THE HOME
right
Painter Charlotte Culot bought her old range from a local village in Provence. The charcoal-burning stove helps warm the room in winter.

TEA BREAK left

A portable single gas burner is just the right size to hold a kettle of water for making tea.

LABELED UP above
Any lettering on an item, especially if in a foreign language, can add a great deal to its charm.

PICKLED WOOD left
The woodwork in this kitchen has been "aged" by the addition of white paint sanded smooth.

(though any sign of damage means they are not safe actually to cook with), while old stove-top kettles, wooden utensils, salt-glazed storage jars, and chunky earthenware pottery can be stowed on open shelves until needed.

Secondhand ranges are highly prized for their warmth, good looks, and efficiency, but prices tend to reflect the keen demand for machines in sound working condition, so always seek the advice of a qualified professional before having one installed to make sure that you are spending your money wisely.

For a slightly more sophisticated kitchen, a different sort of junk sets the tone. Choose an old ceramic sink and simple pieces of furniture painted in shades of warm cream, pale blue, and soft green. Tongue-and-groove wall paneling looks lovely when given the same treatment. Line shelves with rows of tins and enamelware, or display an assortment of delicately patterned dishes on wall-mounted plate racks and simple cup hooks—all will contribute more to the room's style and mood than their modest price tag might suggest.

In addition to being decorative, old cans can be restored to their original purpose and be used to store anything from dried fruit to flour. Other groceries can be stored in old meat lockers, wooden crates, baskets, metal buckets, and even large preserving pans.

Keep cleaning materials out of sight under the sink, concealed by a simple curtain made by gathering some old fabric on a length of wire.

IN THE BALANCE
right
Traditional commercial weighing scales have a reliable quality.

LITTLE PITCHERS
below
Pitchers are invaluable around the kitchen for serving ice water or holding flowers.

OLD AND NEW
above

A quirky collection of junk containers adds character to a restrained contemporary kitchen.

A UNIFIED WHOLE
right

An accumulation of interesting finds has been put together in this kitchen to create a room full of personality.

GOOD SERVICE
above left and left

The best junk finds earn their keep by being functional as well as looking good.

bedrooms

Your bedroom should be as relaxed and comfortable as any other room in your home—if not more so. Filling a bedroom with junk-store finds will strike just the right balance between indulgence and simplicity. Imagine a plain wrought-iron bed made up with white cotton sheets and covered with a downy quilt, and you willl appreciate the essence of this style.

DISPLAY left
This beautifully battered linen closet was painted to match the monochrome decorative scheme.

ORNATE IRON this page
The bed came from a flea market in Belgium; its linen was found at Provence's Isle sur la Sorgue market.

FIELD OF DREAMS
above
Large furniture sales are the best place to go to find a range of antique beds in one place.

DORMITORY
above right
These iron beds began life in a boarding school. You may find similar ones in salvage yards—or check the local press for announcements of closing-down sales at schools or nursing homes.

Battered antique bedsteads appear in all the usual junk-lovers' haunts, and each will create a slightly different mood and style in your bedroom. Sometimes headboards are available together with their bases, mattresses, or footboards, sometimes without. However, don't pass over a beautiful find simply because it is incomplete, since separate bases and mattresses can easily be bought or made to fit. Falling in love with the headboard itself is the most important thing. Remember, too, that the most unusual junk-store finds can be adapted to make headboards—gates, plank doors, and carved panels can all be cut

BRASSED OFF left

Examine painted metal bedsteads carefully—you might find brass hidden under the paint.

OLD LINEN below

Simple bed linen with just a hint of decoration is the best dressing for an ornate bed.

GATEWAY
this page

Think beyond the obvious in the bedroom. Weathered wooden gates make quirky head- and footboards.

WELL HANDLED
opposite

Don't be finicky about cleaning up your find. Accessories, such as handles, and flaking paint can add to the charm.

to size and fitted to a base, so keep your mind open to such possibilities while engaged in your search.

Simple metal-framed hospital and dormitory beds are good for children because of their sturdiness, while more decorative wrought-iron versions, singles or doubles, are ideal for guest rooms. More intricate designs—perhaps a *lit bateau* or a bed with brass knobs—

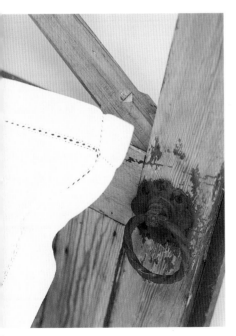

might be worth reserving for a master bedroom, where a hint of grandeur can be beautifully offset by the room's humbler elements. A romantic four-poster is a rare junk-store discovery, but you could make your own version using reclaimed or recycled wooden supports and draping them with plain white voile curtains.

The bedroom is an excellent place to mix old with new: the charm of an old frame with the comfort of a modern mattress, or a vintage cotton cover on a new comforter. When buying new pillows and quilts, opt for ones that are filled in the traditional manner with duck feathers or, better still, goose down.

Bedroom furniture can be as minimal or as decorative as you like. Near-empty rooms that contain just a bed make a dramatic statement and are somehow deeply appealing. But bear in mind that the peace and tranquility of this sort of space will quickly be shattered by too much clutter, so avoid this look unless you are impeccably neat, own very few possessions, or have space for a separate dressing room. A less austere solution is to introduce several pieces of junk furniture. Store clothes in a wooden armoire, as large as you have space for, a chest of drawers, or a linen chest; an alternative is to use a commercial metal clothes rack bought from a wholesale supplier or picked up in a junk sale. When looking for bedside tables, think beyond conventional cabinets and use small round metal café tables, wooden stools, or metal seats to allow you to keep your water glass and nighttime reading close at hand.

ORIGINAL FEATURES
below
These walls, in a house dating from 1520, have been left virtually as they were discovered after 30 years of neglect.

TRAVELING BED right
This 1860s traveling bed was found, covered with baggage labels, in an English antiques shop.

BATHING IN STYLE
right
This bath traveled on the top of a car from a Brussels flea market to its home in Provence. An old wooden frame found on a farm has become a quirky towel rack.

SHATTERED GLASS
left
A fragment of mirror perched on the faucets is all that's needed.

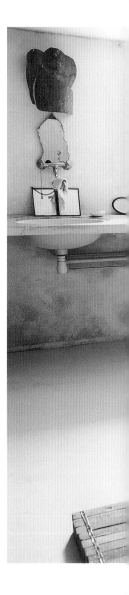

bathrooms

Serious junk-shoppers find it difficult to resist reclaimed antique bathroom fixtures. Cast-iron rolltop clawfoot bathtubs are far superior to flimsy modern acrylic versions, for example. The same goes for old porcelain sinks set in metal stands, huge chrome daisy-head shower attachments, and Victorian toilets with their original high-mounted cisterns.

A few small alterations can make all the difference to existing plain white fixtures. For example, you could swap the faucets for reconditioned originals, introduce some down-to-earth junk-style accessories, and whitewash your bathroom walls. Then all that remains for you to do is to fill the tub, immerse yourself in warm water, lie back, and relax.

SAFELY STORED
this page
Bathrooms are ideal places for showing off all those wonderful pieces of china you've collected. A classic white jug will find a home anywhere, while pretty plates can hold small items of bathroom paraphernalia.

LIGHT AND AIRY
opposite
A charming basin has been tucked into the eaves of this Normandy barn. The mirror has been sliced to fit the space neatly.

Infinite variety is available to those who search architectural salvage yards and specialized outlets at home and abroad in pursuit of something unique. Stumbling on an old bathtub used as a cattle trough in the middle of a field is less likely to happen these days—but you might get lucky. Re-enameling the bath is always possible if it is otherwise in good shape.

Devotees of junk style do not mind having a sink, bathtub, and toilet that don't match. Nor do they object to using a garden table as a washstand, as long as the spirit of casual simplicity reigns. So mix different styles, designs and functions according to what is available and what looks best.

Once you have established the look of the bathroom with its main fixtures, try to keep everything else as simple and uncluttered as possible. To maintain the bathroom's clean lines, a surprising amount of storage space is required. Pieces of furniture imported from elsewhere in the house can all find a home here: store toiletries in a spare

kitchen cabinet, hang bathrobes on an peg rack brought up from the pantry, or pile towels into an empty blanket box from the bedroom.

Traditional-style items of bathroom furniture are as useful as they ever were, so when you go shopping keep your eyes open for old lockable medicine chests, small mirrored cabinets, and tile-backed washstands. For authenticity's

glass tumbler to hold the toothbrushes, a floral-patterned china saucer as a soap dish, or a basic wooden trestle as a towel rack. Similarly, if you can't find a bath mat made in the old-fashioned way from cork or wooden duckboard slats, use a small hearth rug instead.

Flowers give as much pleasure in the bathroom as they do in any other room, so put a small vase containing a few stems on the washstand bathroom shelf, or hang up a bunch of lavender to keep the air fresh and sweet-smelling. Such small details will enhance the sensual pleasure of your bathroom.

sake, combine them with an enameled or porcelain pitcher and bowl set and piles of embroidered cotton handtowels.

Classic bathroom accessories, such as glass shelves, mirrors, shaving mugs, toothbrush holders, soap dishes, and heated chrome towel rods, also appear from time to time in flea markets. Otherwise, you can improvise with a piece of driftwood as a shelf, a gold-framed hall mirror above the sink, a old

ALL AT SEA
this page
*Toy ships from a
secondhand furniture
warehouse give this
room a seagoing theme.*

NAUTICAL SINK
opposite, left
*This buy, from a seaside
junk store, was once
owned by a sea captain.*

SALVAGE JOB
opposite, right
*With a little work,
enameled sinks can
be restored to life.*

CROSSED WIRES
opposite, above left
Twisted-metalwork
containers are ideal for
holding bathroom items,
since they allow water
to drain away.

SOAP STARS
opposite, below left and
above right
Enamelware dishes
come in all shapes, even
shells. Lettering makes
them more collectible.

SINKING FEELING
opposite, below left
Look for unusually
shaped basins—industrial
designs are frequently
more interesting than
domestic ones.

REINVENTION
this page
This lovely enameled
dish, formerly an ashtray,
is far more suitably
employed holding
blocks of soap.

TROUGH
right and above

The unusually deep tub in this elegant paneled bathroom is actually a cattle trough that was found abandoned in a field. The wooden feet were made specially to support it, and the faucets have been fixed to the wall to avoid damaging the tub.

SHIP AHOY
far right

White-painted walls and white tiles maximize the light from an old ship's lamp—a characterful accent in a bathroom.

workrooms,
studios, and studies

Whether you run a business from home or just need a place to write letters, pay bills, pursue hobbies, or store papers, a workspace is essential. Filling your study with modern office furniture would make it efficient, neat, and well-organized, but its dull uniformity and lack of character would leave much to be desired. Turn instead to junk and you can create a space with style, flair, and a distinctly human touch. Even in the most minimal environment, a few quirky, characterful pieces will be inspirational.

First, choose a location. If you have a whole room at your disposal, it's relatively easy to create a business-like workspace—with the advantage of being able to shut the door on everything at the end of the day. For a less spacious office, but one that can still accommodate a small writing table, use part of a wide landing or the corner of a bedroom or dining room.

First on your shopping list should be a work table. A old rolltop desk can be ideal, especially one with lots of built-in

WORKSTATION
opposite and below
Surround yourself with stylish accessories while you work to create an atmosphere conducive to concentration.

WINDOW SEATS
above and right
*Small tables used as
impromptu desks make
the most of the natural
light streaming in
through the windows.*

drawers, letter racks, and pen holders. But this sort of piece is not cheap, and a simple kitchen table or console may do just as well. If your studio is used for practical work, such as painting or sewing, a wooden trestle—or even an old door resting on two low cupboards —will more than suffice. A comfortable seat, ideally one that is adjustable and provides good back support, is the next priority. Look for chairs that were originally intended for office use. It seems appropriate to restore such furniture to its primary function; and by its very nature, good office furniture will have been designed to provide long-lasting comfort.

In addition to finding out when office-furniture clearance sales are due to take place in your area, you can also check out sales and auctions for older styles, such as adjustable architects' chairs with low back supports and wooden swivel chairs on castors—they still look great and their classic clean lines work well in a modern, junk-style environment.

You need to devise ingenious storage solutions to keep documents, stationery, materials, equipment, and books under control—especially if space is limited. Many people find that they work best in uncluttered surroundings. Shelving is essential—whether you use lengths of bare plank and some old bricks, or find an inexpensive bookcase in a junk store. Office-furniture clearance sales are also an excellent source of pieces such as solid-wood filing cabinets, plain metal drawer units, large map chests, and old metal lockers.

For smaller-scale organization, you can use an old vase as a pen holder, leather trunks for filing paperwork, baskets as in-trays, and hatboxes for stowing any other odds and ends.

It is hard to disguise the unattractive look of equipment such as fax machines and computers, but an old typewriter or a reconditioned Bakelite telephone will help to redress the balance and prevent high-tech styling from taking over totally.

Adjustable gooseneck desk lamps, also reminiscent of another era, remain extremely practical and stylish options for all kinds of close work.

WORK WITH A VIEW
above
The most basic wooden table can be turned into an inviting desk. Drawers *are a useful feature for the storage of small stationery items, while an interesting outlook adds to the appeal.*

INSIDE OUT left
*This outbuilding-turned-
garden room is filled with
plants, ladders, pots, and
straw hats in wonderfully
organized chaos.*

sunrooms
and greenhouses

A sense of the natural world—with its wonderful colors and scents and its graceful dust and decay—is the overwhelming atmosphere in a greenhouse.

Carry an old wooden bench out here to work on—it can double as a makeshift dining table in the cooler months of the year when the garden is out of bounds. Start a collection of old gardening tools, and either hang them from hooks and nails or lean them in a corner ready for use. Along with the plants, work-smoothed baskets, gardening gloves, shears, shovels, spades, and forks are the only decoration your sunroom needs.

POTTED HISTORY right
*Timeworn terracotta,
wood, clay, and painted
brick give a potting shed
traditional appeal.*

**UNDER GLASS far
right, above and below**
*A flourishing potting
shed can be a place
of activity as well as
somewhere to relax.*

LOOKING IN above
Plenty of greenery, both inside and out, give a subdued and romantic atmosphere to this barn set in an orchard.

BENCH MARK left
Redolent of traditional skills, even the most ordinary workbench can become an understated decorative feature.

OLD WORLD opposite, above and below
A covered studio next to a converted barn is filled with weathered furniture and the artist-owner's own canvasses.

living outdoors

Any patch of yard, however small, can become an outdoor haven in fine weather. Even a narrow balcony or the smallest paved area beside the back door is room enough for a small marble-topped table and white-painted metal chairs where you can eat breakfast or lunch on a summer's day. Furnish it accordingly, treating it with the same care and making use of junk style just as you would inside the home. Just as you can happily use garden furniture indoors, by the same token you can transfer furniture originally designed for the home to an outdoor setting. The visible effects of aging—such a key part of the appeal of junk style—are accelerated when furniture is

directly exposed to the elements. And if you have picked up an old table and some chairs at little cost, you will not be particularly upset when the paint blisters or lichens make their home in the cracks of bare wood. Even fabrics can be left to take their chances—for example, deckchair canvas can be allowed to bleach in the sun until its gaudy stripes have faded to shadows.

One great pleasure of outdoor living—and one of the most enjoyable ways of

SUMMER LIFE
left

*A semicovered area
sheltered from the
elements is used as a
seasonal dining room.*

AL FRESCO DELIGHTS
above and far left

*Take lunch or dinner in
the shade of a leafy tree.
Hurricane lamps will give
light as dusk falls.*

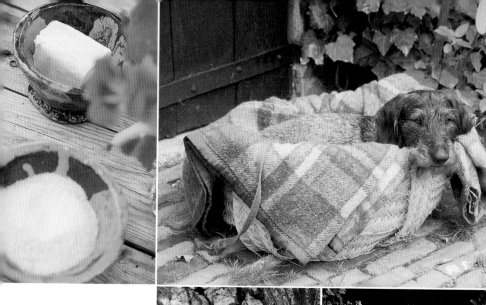

GARDEN DISPLAY
above and right

Outdoor ornamentation takes many forms, from the pleasingly practical to the purely decorative. Visible signs of decay are an optional extra.

A DOG'S LIFE
above right

Even animals can enjoy the benefits of junk style. This contented canine surveys outdoor activities from the comfort of a recycled basket.

TIMEWORN left, below left and above right

Outdoor furniture should not be too delicate—choose pieces with a weathered look to add to the sense of informality.

DAY BED below

Piled with pillows and blankets to soften the hard metal, this ironwork lounger makes a quiet place to relax and enjoy the scenery.

*Lunch is served outside
in a part of the orchard
surrounding the house
of artist Yuri Kuper. The
tables and chairs were
designed by Kuper;
their wooden surfaces
have been allowed to
mellow with age and a
covering of lichen.*

ABANDONED IN SITU
below

*Reminder of a bygone
age, a forgotten plow
lies rusting in a field.*

relaxing with friends—is dining outside. Choose a sheltered
position for your garden table and chairs—this could be on the
lawn, in a cobbled clearing at the bottom of the garden, or
closer to the house on a terrace or veranda. So that you can
enjoy al fresco meals in the heat of the midday sun, make sure
there is some shade—an old parasol, a canopy of vines, or a
shady tree will all do the job.

Junk dining furniture made from metal, rattan, wicker, or wood
is ideal. If it is slightly faded, rusted, or weather-worn to start with,
so much the better. Either leave a wooden tabletop on show or
throw a simple checked cloth or white sheet over it, adding
generously filled pitchers of garden flowers to capture the lazy
mood of high summer. Add plenty of soft pillows covered in

easygoing cotton if your chairs are not as comfortable as they might be; alternatively, you could make some oversized covers from an assortment of remnants and keep a spare set to wrap around your living-room pillows when needed.

Set the table with the same pieces you would use for indoor dining. None of your robust glass tumblers, worn linen napkins, flea-market china plates, or odd pieces of flatware is too precious for a trip into the garden, and all are far more attractive than the usual plastic knives and forks or paper plates and cups.

To allow your guests to make the most of the occasion far into the evening, hang hurricane lamps and storm lanterns in the trees and light them as dusk falls. Less expensive and easier still are old jars with plain white candles inside, protected from any stray breezes.

The relaxed way in which it adapts to life in the garden demonstrates how versatile junk style can be. Who would swap the ease with which possessions can be transferred from house to garden and back again for the tensions and restrictions of conventional living?

SEA VIEW opposite

When you live as close as this to the sea, the beach may become your yard, so try to use sympathetic materials such as reclaimed wood.

FRESH AIR
left and above

Traditional wooden deck chairs with unbleached canvas seats let visitors enjoy the sea breeze in comfort and style.

living outdoors **139**

resources

MARKETS AND FAIRS

When traveling, call the area Chamber of Commerce for information about local flea markets.

Aloha Flea Market

9500 Salt Lake Boulevard
(in the parking lot of Aloha Stadium)
Honolulu, HA
tel: 808-730-9611
Held every Wednesday, Saturday, and Sunday. For more than 20 years, this market has catered to the eclectic tastes of America's westernmost residents and their visitors.

All-American Trade Day

11190 U.S. Highway 413
(between Albertville and Gunterville)
Gunterville, AL
tel: 205-891-2790
Held weekends all year. In addition to collectibles, this indoor and outdoor market sells livestock, poultry, and fresh produce.

American Park'n'Swap

40th Street and Washington Street
Phoenix, AZ
tel: 602-273-1258
www.americanparknswap.com
Held every Wednesday evening, Friday, Saturday, and Sunday. The markt's slogan is "everything you can think of from A to Z" and it is true!

Anderson Jockey Lot and Farmer's Market

Highway 29 North
Belton, SC
tel: 864-224-2027
Every weekend. Produce and livestock as well as all sorts of vintage items.

The Annex Antiques Fair and Flea Market

Sixth Avenue from 24th to 27th Streets
New York, NY
tel: 212-243-5343
Two parking lots turn into flea markets every Saturday and Sunday all year long. Other lots, indoors and out, have joined, and the whole area blossoms with vintage and antique stuff.

Brimfield Antiques and Collectibles

Brimfield, MA
tel: 413-245-3436
www.brimfieldshow.com
Held first week of May, July, and September. Dealers come from all over—including Europe—bringing everything from large pieces of furniture to silver to vintage linens.

Broadacres Swap Meet

2930 Las Vegas Boulevard North
(at Pecos Street)
North Las Vegas, NV
tel: 702-642-3777
www.broadacresswapmeet.com
Held every Friday, Saturday, and Sunday all year long, this outdoor flea market is the oldest and largest in Nevada. Look for "treasures" that have relocated to the Southwest with their owners, as well as local items.

Colorado Springs Flea Market

5225 East Platte Avenue (Highway 24)
Colorado Springs, CO
tel: 719-380-8599
www.csfleamarket.com
Held every Saturday and Sunday year-round as well as Fridays from June through September. This outdoor market has the tang of the Old West.

Englishtown Auction Sales

90 Wilson Avenue
Englishtown, NJ
tel: 732-446-9644
Held every Saturday and Sunday all year. Also open on special holidays and the five days before Christmas.

Flea Market at Eastern Market

Seventh Street, SE at Eastern Market
(half block from Pennsylvania Avenue on Capitol Hill)
Washinton, DC
tel: 703-534-7612
www.easternmarket.net
Held Sundays from March through Christmas. This market has a real old-fashioned neighborhood charm along with the international atmosphere the area provides.

Fort Lauderdale Swap Shop

3291 W. Sunrise Boulevard
Fort Lauderdale, FL
tel: 954-791-7927
Held every day of the year from 6.00 a.m. to 6.00 p.m. Professional dealers and locals exhibit a wide variety of secondhand items.

French Market: Community Flea Market

1235 North Peters Street
(Elysian Fields at the Mississippi River)
New Orleans, LA
tel: 504-596-3420
Held daily out-of-doors, weather permitting. In place since the 18th century, this market represents New Orleans's fancy but faded decorating style.

Hartville Marketplace and Flea Market

1289 Edison Street NW
Hartville, OH
tel: 330-877-9860
www.hartvillefleamarket.com
Held Mondays, Thursdays, and Saturdays, April. Look out for the Amish and Mennonite food purveyors as well as dealers in all sorts of merchandise.

Hinckley Flea Market

803 Highway 48 at I-35
Hinckley, MN
tel: 320-384-9911
Operates weekly from May to September, Thursdays through Sunday. This is Minnesota's most modern market.

Jack Loeks' Flea Market

1400 28th Street SW
(three miles west of Route 131, in the Studio 28 parking lot)
Grand Rapids, MI
tel: 616-532-8218
Held every weekend from April through October, rain or shine. For 30 years this outdoor antiques and collectibles flea market has been selling all sorts of attic treasures and soon-to-be collectibles.

Kane County Flea Market

Rt. 64 and Randall Road
St. Charles, IL
tel: 630-377-2252
www.kanecountyfleamarket.com
Held every second Sunday, from May
through October. Indoor and outdoor
booths specializing in heartland
antiques and collectibles.

Lakewood Antiques Market

2000 Lakewood Way
Atlanta, GA
tel: 404-622-4488
www.lakewoodantiques.com
Held every Friday, Saturday, and
Sunday on the second full weekend of
each month. Antiques, collectibles, and
rediscovered treasures are the only
things featured here.

Long Beach Outdoor Antiques and Collectibles Market

Veteran Boulevard at Lakewood
Boulevard
Long Beach, CA
tel: 213-655-5703
www.longbeachantiquemarket.com
Held the third Sunday of every month.
A wide variety of merchandise from
regular dealers and private individuals.

Mary's Ole TIme Swap Meet

7925 Northeast 23rd Street
Oklahoma City, OK
tel: 405-427-0051
Held every weekend year-round.

Picc-a-dilly Flea Market

796 West 13th Street (Lane County
Fairgrounds)
Eugene, OR
tel: 541-683-5589
Held first and third Sundays of every
month. Since 1970 this flea market
has attracted dealers from all over
selling a wide variety of antiques and
collectibles.

Redwood Swap Meet

3688 Redwood Road
Salt Lake City, UT
tel: 801-973-6060
Held every Saturday and Sunday,
weather permitting. This market
offers a wide variety of collectibles
and vintage items.

Renningers Market

740 Noble Street
Kutztown, PA
tel: 717-385-0104
www.renningers.com
Held every Friday and Saturday
year-round. Amish, Pennsylvania
Dutch, primitive, and folk art are
the specialties, but you will find
lots of everything.

The Rose Bowl Flea Market

Pasadena, CA
tel: 626-588-4411
Held the second Sunday of every
month.Vintage goods from high kitsch
to fine furnishings.

Tennessee State Fairgrounds Flea Market

Wedgewood Avenue and
Nolensville Road
(State Fairgrounds)
Nashville, TN
tel: 615-862-5016
Held the fourth weekend of every
month, except December, when the
maket is held on the third weekend.
This flea market is a long-established
Nashville tradition.

Traders Village

7979 North Eldridge Parkway
Houston, TX
tel: 281-890-5500
www.tradersvillage.com
Held every weekend year-round.

STORES & DESIGNERS

280 Modern

280–284 Lafayette Street
New York, NY 10012
tel: 212-941-5825

Annette Brederode

Lynbaans-gracht 56d
Amsterdam
The Netherlands
(by appointment)

Anthropologie

375 West Broadway
New York, NY 10012
tel: 212-343-7070
www.anthropologie.com

Arne Maynard Garden Design

Clerkenwell House
125 Golden Lane
London EC1 0TJ
UK
tel: +44-(0)20-7689-8100
www.arne-maynard.com

Caroline's Antiek and Brocante

Nieuweweg 35A
1251 LH Laren
The Netherlands
tel: 035 531 23 73

Clifton Nurseries

5a, Clifton Villas
London W9 2PH
UK
tel: +44-(0)20-7289-6851
www.clifton.co.uk

Fishs Eddy

889 Broadway
New York, NY 10011
tel: 212-420-2090
www.fishseddy.com

John Langdon

Benefold Farm
Petworth
West Sussex GU28 9NX
UK
tel: + 44-(0)179-834-4066
(expert barn relocation)

Peter Hone

5 Ladbroke Square
London W11 3LX
UK
(Gardens antique consultant;
by appointment only)

Potted Gardens

41 King Street
New York, NY 10014
tel: 212-255-4797

Ruby Beets Antiques

1703 Montauk Highway
Bridgehampton, NY 11932
tel: 516-537-2802

Xavier Nicod et Gérard Nicod

9 av. des Quatre Otages
L'Isle-sur-la-Sorgue
France
tel: + 33-4-90-38-35-50

index

acknowledgments

My thanks go to Tom Leighton, for his kindness and good humor and for always taking beautiful pictures whatever the weather, and to Simon Whitmore, his assistant, for keeping us on the right road. Also to Larraine Shamwana, for her consistent encouragement and great art direction—her huge contribution to pulling this project together creatively will not be forgotten.

Junk Style would not have come together at all without the wonderful houses we were allowed to photograph, so I am indebted to their owners, all of whom seemed to share the same spirit and made the photography for this book so memorable: garden antiques expert Peter Hone, garden designer Arne Maynard, interior designer Philip Hooper, artist Yuri Kuper, painter Charlotte Culot, lighting designer Alexis Aufray, designers Roxanne Beis and Jean-Bernard Navier; and also Marilyn Phipps, Netty Nauta, Caroline and Michael Breet, Aleid Rontgen and Annette Brederode; Glen Senk and Keith Johnson of Anthropologie, Jim and Pat Cole of Coming to America, and George Laaland at Woolloomooloo Restaurant. I am also grateful to the following stores for kindly allowing us to photograph their wonderful collections of secondhand furniture and accessories: Xavier Nicod Antiquites, 9 Avenue des Quatre, Otages, 84800 Isle sur la Sorgue, France; Anthropologie, 375 West Broadway, New York, NY 10012; 201 West Lancaster Avenue, Wayne, PA 19087; 11500 Rockville Pike, Rockville, MD 20852; 1365 Post Road East, Westport, CT 06880; 9 Northern Boulevard, Greenvale, NY 11548; 823 Newport Center Drive, Newport Beach, CA 92660, 1402 Third Street Promenade, Santa Monica, CA 90401; 1120 North State Street, Chicago, IL 60610; 1780 Green Bay Road, Highland Park, IL 60035; Coming to America, 276 Lafayette Street, New York, NY 10012; Fishs Eddy, 889 Broadway, New York , NY 10003 and 2176 Broadway, New York, NY 10024; Potted Gardens, 27 Bedford Street, New York, NY 10014 and Bridgehampton, NY 11932; Ruby Beets Antiques, 1703 Montauk Highway, Bridgehampton, NY 11932. I would also like to thank all my friends and colleagues who helped me locate the stores, especially Polly and Mark Gilbey in London, Roxanne Beis, and Amelie Thiodet in France, Nina Monfils in Holland, and Andrea Raisfeld in New York.

Thanks to my sister Caroline for her translations, to Fiona Craig McFeely and Jo Tyler for their help, to my agent Fiona Lindsay, and to all at Ryland Peters & Small. Thanks also to my brilliant sons, George and Ralph, for taking my too frequent absences in such good humor, and to Belinda, for keeping things together at home. Above all, thanks to my wonderful husband, Martin, for everything.